Who Was Abigail Adams?

Who Was Abigail Adams?

by True Kelley

illustrated by John O'Brien

Grosset & Dunlap
An Imprint of Penguin Random House

For Eloise and Charlotte Lindblom—TK

For my daughter Terase—JOB

GROSSET & DUNLAP
Penguin Young Readers Group
An Imprint of Penguin Random House LLC

Library of Congress Cataloging-in-Publication Data is available.

ISBN 978-0-448-47890-6   10 9 8 7

Contents

Who Was
Abigail Adams?

On June 17, 1775, at 3:00 a.m., Abigail Adams woke up with a start. Her bed was shaking. The dull boom of cannons ten miles away in Boston shook the whole house. The British and the American colonists were at war. Abigail had almost gotten used to hearing the boom from cannons every day as the armies fought.

But this time was different. The cannon fire went on and on and on.

Abigail's first thoughts were for the safety of her four children. She had managed the Adamses' small farm and big family by herself for months because her husband, John, was away. He had been nervous about leaving his family in a danger zone. However, he and Abigail both felt that he had to be at an important meeting in Philadelphia. John was among a growing number of people who wanted the colonies to break free from British rule. The meeting would decide the future of the thirteen American colonies.

At daybreak, Abigail and her seven-year-old son, John Quincy, climbed the hill behind their house to see what was happening. They could hear the guns roaring even louder. They stood on a pile of rocks at the top to get a better view.

What they saw was horrifying. Beyond the British warships in Boston Harbor, flames and

black smoke rose above the city. Abigail and her
son held hands and walked down the hill in tears.

The battle was one of the most important of the
Revolutionary War—the Battle of Bunker Hill.

Soon Abigail wrote about it to her husband. John showed her letters to General George Washington, the new head of the American army.

GEORGE WASHINGTON

Abigail was living in amazing times, and she described them and her life in amazing letters: She wrote over three thousand letters in her lifetime!

Abigail and her husband, John, had a special
bond. You'll see that if you read their letters to
each other. They both were deeply interested
in politics. Abigail always thought first of her
husband and family. But she was strongly for
the rights of women, for education, and against
slavery. She had many ideas about what freedom
meant. She made sure her important husband
heard her!

THE RIGHT TO AN EDUCATION

ABIGAIL BELIEVED EDUCATION WAS VERY IMPORTANT. SHE SENT ONE OF HER BLACK SERVANTS, A STABLE BOY NAMED JAMES, TO SCHOOL IN QUINCY. THIS WAS NEVER DONE, AND PEOPLE PROTESTED. OTHER BOYS REFUSED TO GO TO SCHOOL IF JAMES DID. ABIGAIL TOLD THEM, "BECAUSE HIS FACE IS BLACK, IS HE TO BE DENIED INSTRUCTION?" JAMES ATTENDED THE SCHOOL WITH NO FURTHER PROTEST.

Abigail lived apart from John for many years. She suffered the hardships of war, political defeats, and the deaths of three of her children. But she stayed strong through it all, and her strength helped both her husband and her son John Quincy to become presidents of the United States.

Abigail Adams was a great woman in her own right, a woman clearly ahead of her times.

Chapter 1
Young Abigail

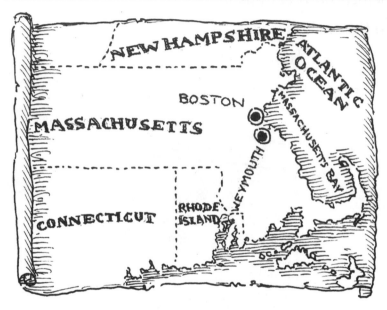

Abigail Smith was born in Weymouth, Massachusetts, on November 11, 1744. Her mother, Elizabeth Quincy Smith, came from a respected family. Abigail's father, William Smith, was a much-admired minister. Abigail had a

brother, William, and two sisters, Mary and
Elizabeth. She was close to her sisters all her life.

Abigail was delicate and sickly when she was little. She didn't go to school. Most girls in those days didn't, even though boys did. Abigail thought it was very unfair that her brother could go to school and she couldn't. She found out early that girls in colonial America didn't have the same rights as boys.

But Abigail and her sisters were lucky. Their
mother taught them reading, writing, and
arithmetic, as well as how to cook and sew. Their
father and grandfather both had big libraries.
Abigail was a curious child, and she spent a lot

of time with her nose in all those books. Abigail read Shakespeare's plays, history, philosophy and law. Her mother worried that she read too

much. She also worried that Abigail was too stubborn and strong-willed. Grandmother Quincy

always was on Abigail's side, though. She said,
"Wild colts make the best horses."

Visitors often gathered in the Smiths' library
to borrow books and to talk about politics. A war
against the French was being fought along the
frontier borders of the colonies. Also, a new king
in England was making trouble for the colonists.
Everyone had different ideas of what should be

done. Abigail listened in. Girls weren't usually allowed to speak openly, but Abigail's father encouraged it. Abigail was shy, yet she did have opinions, and sometimes she spoke up.

One visitor to the Smith's home was a young lawyer, John Adams. The first time he met Abigail, she was fifteen. He was twenty-four. At first, they didn't like each other that much. Abigail thought he was dumpy looking, moody, self-centered, and he talked too much. John thought Abigail didn't talk enough! But over time, as John kept visiting, he and Abigail got to know each other better. They both had lively minds. They thought alike and loved politics. Slowly they fell in love. It was a love that lasted for fifty-seven years.

YOUNG JOHN ADAMS

JOHN ADAMS WAS BORN ON OCTOBER 30, 1735, IN WHAT IS NOW QUINCY, MASSACHUSETTS. HE HAD TWO YOUNGER BROTHERS. HIS MOTHER, SUSANNA BOYLSTON ADAMS, WAS FROM A WELL-KNOWN FAMILY. HIS FATHER WAS A FARMER, AND JOHN WAS VERY CLOSE TO HIM. HE WAS VERY PROUD TO BE THE SON OF A FARMER. WHEN HE WAS SIXTEEN, JOHN WENT TO HARVARD COLLEGE. AFTERWARD HE TAUGHT SCHOOL FOR A FEW YEARS. THEN HE DECIDED TO BE A LAWYER. IN 1764, WHEN HE WAS ALMOST TWENTY-NINE, HE MARRIED ABIGAIL SMITH.

Chapter 2
A New Family

Abigail's mother and father didn't think John Adams was good enough for Abigail. They didn't like that he came from a family of farmers. But when Abigail was almost twenty and John was almost twenty-nine, Abigail's parents changed their minds and let them marry in the Smith family home.

After the ceremony they rode to their first home in nearby Braintree. It was a small saltbox house and farm right next door to where John had been born and raised. Their house was called a "saltbox" because it looked like a type of wooden box used to store salt in those days. The house had a sloping roof with two stories in the front and only one story in the back.

Though John was a lawyer, he loved farming. Abigail loved being a farm wife: cooking, sewing, spinning, churning butter, smoking meats, gardening, and caring for the sheep, chickens, and cows.

Soon Abigail was a mother, too. Nabby (Abigail) was born in 1765. Two years later, John Quincy was born. The Adamses hired help,

but the days were still full for Abigail. She also managed to get up early or stay up late to write letters to friends and family. Even as a young girl, Abigail had loved writing letters to people close to her. One of the few times in her life when she stopped writing was in 1770, when their baby girl, Susanna, died.

John often had to be away from home. His
law practice took him all over New England. He
was also speaking out against British taxes that
Americans had to pay. Most of all, colonists like

John Adams were furious over the Stamp Act, which was a tax on most printed materials. With John away, Abigail was left home to take charge, and she did it very well. But she was lonely.

In 1768, the Adams family moved to Boston so John could be nearer to his work. They had a little girl, Susanna, who, sadly, died in 1770. She was only a year old. Both John and Abigail were broken-hearted. That same year their son Charles was born, and in 1772 they had another son, Thomas.

Abigail was excited to be in big, busy Boston.
There were lots of shops and four newspapers.
Her sister lived there, and so did Abigail's friend

MERCY WARREN

Mercy Warren.
But British
soldiers were
everywhere on
the lookout for
trouble from
the colonists.
Bostonians
didn't like that.
Sometimes
Boston felt like
a dangerous
place. The Adamses moved back and forth from
the city to Braintree several times. Tensions were
building.

In protest, Americans stopped buying things
taxed by the British. A tax on tea made Americans

tra mad. They loved tea. Once the tax took effect, Abigail started making her own tea from berry leaves. Lots of people were doing this. It was called "liberty tea." In 1773 a group called the Sons of Liberty protested the tea tax in a famous event that is in all American history books. The men dressed up as Indians and went aboard a tea ship in Boston Harbor. They tossed three hundred chests of tea into the water. This event became known as the Boston Tea Party, and it meant trouble. Big trouble.

THE BOSTON MASSACRE

ON MARCH 5, 1770, A ROWDY MOB STARTED THROWING ICE CHUNKS, OYSTER SHELLS, AND ROCKS AT NINE BRITISH SOLDIERS. FRIGHTENED AND OUTNUMBERED, THE SOLDIERS FIRED INTO THE CROWD. FIVE PEOPLE WERE KILLED AND

OTHERS WOUNDED. REPORTS OF THE INCIDENT, MANY OF THEM INCLUDING "FACTS" THAT WERE UNTRUE, SPREAD THROUGH THE COLONIES. NEWS OF THE MASSACRE HELPED BRING ON THE AMERICAN REVOLUTION FIVE YEARS LATER.

Chapter 3
Trouble Brewing

John and Abigail were happy about the Boston Tea Party. They could see that it was a turning point. More and more colonists wanted freedom from England, even if it meant war.

In 1774, John was elected to go to Philadelphia for the First Continental Congress. Men from the different colonies were to decide what America

should do. Again, Abigail was left to run the household. She wrote to John, but it took two weeks for her letters to reach him. Her letters were full of news and advice. She reported the movements of the British troops. John's letters to her complained about how little was getting done at the Congress. Abigail always called John "dearest friend" in her letters. They missed each other terribly. John missed his children, too.

Abigail wrote in a letter to her friend Mercy Warren that she could see no way to avoid war. She was right.

Shortly after that letter, in April 1775, the British and colonists fought battles in Lexington and Concord, Massachusetts, twenty miles from Braintree. The Revolutionary War had begun. George Washington was put in command of the new Continental Army. From Philadelphia, John wrote to Abigail, "In case of real danger . . . fly to the woods with our children."

In June, after the Battle of Bunker Hill took place across the bay from the farm, Abigail wrote to John. She said, "The constant roar of the cannon is so distressing that we cannot eat, drink, or sleep." Later she found out that one of their closest friends had been killed in the battle.

Can you imagine what it was like to be living in the middle of a war? Abigail sheltered people fleeing Boston and Continental soldiers on their

way into the city. The house was full of friends
and strangers. Abigail fed everyone. They would

sleep in the parlor, the attic, and the barn. Abigail described it as a "scene of confusion."

Because nothing was coming from England, people in Boston were running out of things they needed. Abigail made soap and spun cloth.

She made ink from ashes and berries! She even
melted down pewter spoons to make bullets for
the soldiers.

Money was short. Abigail asked John to send
her six thousand pins. They weren't for her to use.
She wanted to sell them. In the midst of all the
upheaval, she was going into business!

In the summer of 1775 there was a dysentery
epidemic. Dysentery is caused by unclean food
or water, and it hits a person's stomach. Eight of
the Adamses' neighbors died of dysentery in one
week alone. John's brother died, and so did the
Adamses' servant Patty. John and Abigail's three-

year-old son, Thomas, and another servant also got very sick. Abigail's mother came to help nurse everyone. In October, she caught dysentery herself and died.

It was a terrible time. The weather was freezing. The house was cold. Abigail was not the type to complain, but she felt very low, sad, and alone. John's letters comforted her. Still, having her husband far from home was very hard on her sometimes. When he came back from

Philadelphia for a short time at Christmas, John
told Abigail he'd stay home if she wanted him
to. Abigail knew how important his work in the
Congress was. She told him he had to go back.
How difficult that decision must have been!
And how patriotic.

Chapter 4
A New Country Is Born

In January 1776, Abigail again was kept awake all night by the rumble of cannons. The windows rattled all day. The fighting went on for weeks. General George Washington was trying to drive the British out of Boston. Abigail feared the city would be burned down.

In March, from the hill behind her house, she saw a huge fleet of British ships. It was an amazing sight. There were so many ships, Abigail wrote, "They look like a Forrest." One hundred seventy ships had their sails raised. They were leaving the harbor! George Washington had driven out the British! Boston was spared, but the war went on elsewhere.

At that time, John was at the Second

Continental Congress in Philadelphia. He was
working with men from each of the thirteen

colonies on a declaration of independence. It would be a statement that explained why the colonies were breaking away from England.

Abigail wrote to her husband about her beliefs and what she hoped to see in a new American government. Even though her own father still had slaves, Abigail thought there should be no slavery in a free country. She also strongly believed that women should have the same rights as men. In the late 1700s, husbands had total control over their wives. Wives could be treated almost like slaves. Abigail's own drunken brother mistreated his wife, and no one could do anything about it. Abigail wanted laws to protect wives. Women couldn't buy property. They couldn't get the same education as men. In one of her most famous letters to John, Abigail wrote, "Remember the Ladies, and be more generous and favourable to them than your ancestors." She even half-jokingly hinted that women could revolt if they weren't treated more fairly!

John answered, "I cannot but laugh."

Abigail was in Boston in July 1776 when the Declaration of Independence was read to cheering crowds. Church bells rang, guns were fired in the air, and people yelled, "God Save our American

States!" Abigail listened to the reading, but heard nothing about slaves or women. That must have disappointed her greatly. It took until 1865 for slavery to be ended everywhere in the United States. And only in 1920 did women finally get the right to vote.

THE DECLARATION OF INDEPENDENCE

FIVE MEN, INCLUDING JOHN ADAMS, WORKED ON WHAT TO SAY TO KING GEORGE III OF ENGLAND ABOUT THE DEMAND FOR FREEDOM FOR THE THIRTEEN COLONIES. THOMAS JEFFERSON WAS ASKED TO WRITE THAT LETTER, THE DECLARATION OF INDEPENDENCE.

FIFTY-SIX MEN REPRESENTING THE COLONIES, INCLUDING JOHN ADAMS, SIGNED IT. YOU CAN SEE THE ORIGINAL DECLARATION TODAY IN THE NATIONAL ARCHIVES IN WASHINGTON, DC.

In the summer of 1776, another deadly disease spread through New England: smallpox. People were dying. There was a cure, but it was very dangerous. People could have a tiny bit of smallpox virus rubbed into a small cut. They would hopefully get only a mild form of the disease, and then they could never get it again. Often the cure caused blisters that left scars. Sometimes people even died from the cure. It was a terrible chance to take with her children, but Abigail thought the cure was worth trying. Her children did get very sick, but all survived. It was a brave thing for a mother to do. She had to

make the decision, like so many others, by herself.

In February 1777, Congress was forced to move to Baltimore to avoid advancing British troops. John couldn't be with Abigail, even though she was expecting another baby. Abigail didn't feel well. She was afraid she might die in childbirth and leave her children with no mother. Abigail was fine but, sadly, the baby didn't live. Abigail couldn't bear to write John with the terrible news. She later wrote to her husband that they had been married thirteen years "but not more than half that time have we had the happiness of living together." She worried that the children were suffering from his being gone.

Finally, after almost a year away, John returned home. Only a few months later he had to leave again, this time to Paris, all the way across the ocean, to work for peace with England. When he left in February 1778, he took their ten-year-old son, John Quincy, with him.

Chapter 5
Still Apart

John didn't want to leave
Abigail, but she couldn't
go with him to Europe.
She needed to stay home
to run the farm and raise
the children. John also
worried about the dangers
of the trip across the ocean.
Taking his son was risky
enough. As it turned out,
their ship was fired on by a
British ship, outran pirates,
and survived a terrifying
three-day storm. Lightning
killed one of the crew!

Meanwhile, Abigail worried. No one set sail, as John had, in winter. It wasn't safe. And it was wartime! She heard nothing from her husband and son for months. The rumor was that the ship had been captured by the British. Finally, a few letters came to say they were all right, but letters took so long to arrive!

It was a difficult winter for Abigail. There were bad snowstorms in Braintree. War made

everything scarce or expensive. The farm was losing money, and she had to let go some of her help.

Abigail came up with a clever idea. She asked John to send her things she could sell to make money. He did—cloth, tea, dishes, and ribbons, among other things. Abigail had a good head for business. Soon she was ordering items directly from the trading houses in Europe and making a profit. Abigail invested her profits in land and bonds. Many years later, she and her family still lived on this money.

After one and a half years away, John and John Quincy sailed home. They were dropped off from their ship and rowed ashore to Braintree. It came as a complete surprise for Abigail when they appeared at her door!

Unfortunately, the reunion didn't last long.
John had to return to Paris in November 1779.
This time he took not only John Quincy but also
their son Charles. Abigail felt the brothers needed
their father. Still, she described being separated

from her boys as "cruel torture." She was afraid
they'd be gone a very long time. And she was
right. It was almost five years before Abigail saw
her husband and sons again!

John's voyage to Paris was not any easier than
his first trip. The boat was leaky and was forced to
land in Spain. John and his sons had to go eight

hundred miles over land and over mountains to
Paris. They walked or rode mules much of the
way. It took a while. Abigail cried with relief when
she finally got a letter from John. There were
many times after that when Abigail didn't hear
from John for months.

Young Charles was very homesick in Europe and begged to be sent home. He was put on a ship heading back to America. Then there were rumors that Charles' ship was lost. Abigail worried for five months that he was dead, but finally Charles arrived home safely. She felt such relief and happiness!

The war finally came to an end in 1781 when the British surrendered at Yorktown. The thirteen colonies would now become a new independent country, the United States of America. There was so much work to be done to create a new country. What kind of government would it have? What laws?

John Adams was still in Europe when Abigail's father died in September 1783. Abigail had to grieve alone without the comfort of her husband. People in Massachusetts were gossiping about her and John. The Adamses had been apart for so many years. People wondered, How could they love each other? Maybe John had a French girlfriend? Abigail didn't believe the rumors, but her life alone was becoming too much for her.

She begged John to let her join him in Europe. In 1784, she set sail.

NEW LAWS, NEW GOVERNMENT

A GROUP OF MEN KNOWN AS THE FRAMERS WORKED ON FIGURING OUT THE NEW LAWS AND FORM OF GOVERNMENT FOR THE UNITED STATES. IT WAS A VERY BIG JOB! THE FRAMERS DISCUSSED AND ARGUED AND FINALLY COMPROMISED. NO ONE THOUGHT THE NEW GOVERNMENT WAS PERFECT, BUT IT WAS AS GOOD AS THEY COULD DO. THERE WOULD BE THREE BRANCHES OF GOVERNMENT: THE EXECUTIVE (PRESIDENT), JUDICIAL (SUPREME COURT), AND LEGISLATIVE (HOUSE AND SENATE). FINALLY, IN 1789 THE UNITED STATES CONSTITUTION WENT INTO EFFECT, AND BY 1790 ALL THIRTEEN STATES HAD APPROVED IT. IT IS STILL, AFTER MORE THAN TWO HUNDRED YEARS, THE HIGHEST LAW IN THE UNITED STATES.

THE THREE BRANCHES OF GOVERNMENT

EXECUTIVE   LEGISLATIVE   JUDICIAL

Chapter 6
Reunion

Although desperate to see her husband and
son, Abigail dreaded the trip across the ocean. "I
am so much of a coward upon the water," she said.
She would be leaving behind friends and family
whom she might never see again. She put Charles
and young Thomas in the care of her sister. Her
nineteen-year-old daughter, Nabby, was going
with her.

In June 1784, Nabby and Abigail boarded
the ship, the *Active*, with trunks of clothes,

two servants, and a cow. The ship's name was appropriate. It tossed around on the sea. Abigail and Nabby were seasick for days. They couldn't even get out of bed. They were cooped up in a tiny, stuffy, dark cabin. It didn't help that the

ship was dirty. Its cargo of whale oil and potash smelled terrible. The dampness made Abigail's bones and joints hurt. The food was awful. Once she was well enough, Abigail tried to help the cook make better meals. She also got the crew to scrub the floors until they could finally see the boards under the dirt. Abigail wrote, "I am more and more of the mind that a Lady ought Not to go to sea!"

After a month, the ship reached the coast of England. Even then, the trip wasn't over. The passengers were lowered from the ship into a small boat. The waves were six feet high! The small boat was washed up sideways through the roaring surf onto a beach. After that, it took an entire day by carriage to reach London.

ON THE SHIP

IF YOU SAW THE *ACTIVE* TODAY, YOU WOULD THINK IT WAS A VERY SMALL BOAT TO BE CROSSING THE OCEAN. IT WAS A SAILING SHIP BUILT TO CARRY CARGO AND NOT PASSENGERS. THERE WERE ONLY TWO TINY PASSENGER CABINS, BOTH USED BY THE WOMEN.

THE MALE PASSENGERS SLEPT IN THE MAIN
CABIN, WHERE EVERYONE ALSO SAT OR ATE. THE
PASSENGER CABIN DOORS OPENED RIGHT ONTO
THE MAIN CABIN. EVEN WITH THE WINDOWS OPEN,
IT WAS TOO STUFFY TO CLOSE THE DOORS. A
CURTAIN GAVE THE WOMEN SOME PRIVACY, BUT
THEY WAITED TO CHANGE THEIR CLOTHES UNTIL
NO ONE WAS IN THE MAIN CABIN. THAT DIDN'T
HAPPEN OFTEN!

THE CARGO ON THE *ACTIVE* WAS SMELLY
ENOUGH TO MAKE ANYONE SEASICK, EVEN WITHOUT
THE ROCKING OF THE WAVES. WHEN ABIGAIL
WANTED TO GO UP ON DECK TO GET SOME FRESH
AIR, SHE HAD TO BE HELPED BY TWO MEN,
BECAUSE THE BOAT ROCKED SO VIOLENTLY. THEN,
ON DECK, THEY HAD TO TIE HER TO A CHAIR!

In London, Abigail and Nabby were met
by John Quincy. Abigail was shocked to see a
seventeen-year-old man: Her son had been only
twelve when she'd last said good-bye to him. Later,
her husband John arrived. What a joyful reunion!

London was a pleasant surprise for Abigail. It
was sunnier than she had expected. The buildings
were beautiful and the streets were wide. Best of
all, there was indoor plumbing—not outhouses!

The happy Adams family spent three weeks in
London, seeing the sights. Then they crossed the
channel to Paris. John had rented a mansion just
outside the city.

Abigail had loved London. As for Paris, she
thought it was "the very dirtiest place" she had
ever seen. The mansion, however, was another
thing! It was beautiful. It had more than forty

rooms and came with eight servants. There were
huge formal gardens with a fishpond and orange
trees. Their life there was filled with dinner
parties, the opera, museums, theater, and ballet.

The lavish dinner parties of France made
Abigail a little nervous. It was too much! She was
also shocked by the ballet. The costumes were too
skimpy, showing the ballerina's legs much more

than a lady from New England thought proper. It took a while for Abigail Adams to get used to the French ways.

Abigail liked French women because they were smart and free to say what they thought. Still, Abigail missed home, and it was hard not knowing French. She got a pet songbird to keep her company. Then, as had happened so many times before, John had to move because of a new job. He would be the new ambassador to Great Britain. He and Abigail would live in London. Good-bye, pet songbird. Good-bye, Paris. Good-bye, John Quincy, too. He went home to study in America.

John's job in England was difficult. As ambassador, he was expected to make friends with the very people who had recently been at war with America. England was a powerful country, so the United States needed its friendship. When Adams met King George III, they were polite to each other. Nabby and Abigail also met the king. They spent hours getting dressed for the occasion and then waited hours for the king to speak just

a few words to them. They were not very
impressed.

THOMAS JEFFERSON

THOMAS JEFFERSON WAS IN PARIS AT THE SAME TIME AS THE ADAMSES. THEY BECAME VERY GOOD FRIENDS. ABIGAIL EVEN TOOK CARE OF JEFFERSON'S DAUGHTER POLLY WHEN SHE FIRST ARRIVED IN EUROPE TO LIVE WITH HER FATHER IN 1787.

THOMAS JEFFERSON BECAME THE THIRD PRESIDENT OF THE UNITED STATES, RIGHT AFTER JOHN ADAMS. IT WAS AT THAT TIME THAT JEFFERSON AND THE ADAMSES HAD A FALLING OUT OVER POLITICS. THEY BARELY SPOKE TO EACH OTHER FOR YEARS. HOWEVER, WHEN POLLY DIED IN 1804, ABIGAIL ADAMS WROTE TO JEFFERSON IN SYMPATHY. EVENTUALLY, THE FRIENDSHIP WAS RENEWED. THOMAS JEFFERSON AND JOHN ADAMS BECAME VERY CLOSE AGAIN IN THEIR LATER YEARS AND DIED ON THE SAME DAY, JULY 4, 1826. IT WAS EXACTLY FIFTY YEARS AFTER THE SIGNING OF THE DECLARATION OF INDEPENDENCE.

Abigail loved being back in London. She
loved seeing the plays by Shakespeare that she
had first read as a child. She was awestruck when
she heard the beautiful music of Josef Handel

performed. She also loved visiting the countryside and stately homes outside London. On one trip to Southampton, Abigail took her first dip in the sea!

Abigail and John took a long trip to the Netherlands. Abigail admired the simplicity, honesty, and politeness of the people there. Wherever she was, Abigail believed her main job was to help her husband. In England, Mrs. Ambassador arranged dinner parties and diplomatic receptions. She was very good at it. But Abigail and John feared they were gaining weight!

Nabby, meanwhile, married John's handsome secretary, William Smith, in 1786. He had the same name as Abigail's father and brother! The next year they had baby William. Abigail was a grandmother. John was a grandfather.

"A grand—oh no!" she exclaimed. She didn't like to think she was old.

The London newspapers were hard on John. They still hadn't gotten over the war and gave false reports about his speeches. Abigail called them the "News Liars." John felt he was unable to get things done. It was time to go home. By then, Abigail was happy at the thought! It had been almost four years, and she missed her sons Charles and Thomas and her sisters. Also, the Adamses had asked an uncle to buy them a new, larger house in Braintree. It was to be ready for their return.

In March 1788 they began another rough ocean crossing and reached Boston in June. To their surprise, they were greeted in Boston by thousands of cheering people, cannons, and church bells that rang all day. It was a hero's welcome. John and Abigail were overwhelmed.

Best of all, they were finally home . . . together.

Chapter 7
Politics

The new home in Braintree was a big letdown. It was larger than their old house, but compared to the mansion in Paris, it seemed to Abigail like a little "wren's house." It had low ceilings and was dark inside. Also much of their furniture had been

damaged in the ocean crossing. The house needed work—lots of work—if Abigail wanted to turn it into a home. She hired carpenters and masons. She planted roses she brought from England. (They still grow there today.) Their home would be called Peacefield.

Now home, John couldn't resist returning to politics. He was elected to the US Congress. In 1789, in the first presidential election, George Washington got the most votes, but John Adams came in second. In those days, that automatically made John the vice president of the United States. Abigail was the first vice president's wife. So the Adamses were to move again!

New York was the new capital city. Abigail loved their rented mansion that overlooked the Hudson River. Nabby had just had a second baby, John Adams Smith. Her family moved into the mansion with John and Abigail. The Adamses' son Charles, now nineteen years old, was living

there, too, and so was Louisa, the daughter
of Abigail's brother, who had died recently.
Whenever Abigail's children or relatives needed a
place to stay, she took them in. More to the point,
Abigail loved having everyone there. But there
were worries, too. Nabby's husband, William,
was irresponsible and owed people money. John
Quincy was having a hard time starting his law
practice. Charles drank too much. Thomas was
often sick.

WHAT TO CALL THE PRESIDENT

WITH SUCH A NEW GOVERNMENT, NO ONE WAS
SURE WHAT TO CALL THE PRESIDENT. SHOULD HE
BE JUST "MR. WASHINGTON" OR "MR. PRESIDENT"?
OR SHOULD HE BE "EXCELLENCY" OR EVEN "HIS
HIGHNESS THE PRESIDENT OF THE UNITED STATES
OF AMERICA AND PROTECTOR OF THE RIGHTS OF
SAME"? JOHN ADAMS ARGUED THAT THE TITLE
SHOULD BE HONORABLE AND GRAND. HE LIKED
"HIS MAJESTY THE PRESIDENT." ABIGAIL WOULD
NOT HAVE LIKED THAT. SHE DIDN'T BELIEVE IN
FANCY TITLES. THE SENATE ARGUED ABOUT THIS
FOR A MONTH, AND THEIR DECISION MUST HAVE
PLEASED ABIGAIL. SIMPLY "THE PRESIDENT OF THE
UNITED STATES" WAS GOOD ENOUGH. AND PEOPLE
WOULD JUST CALL HIM "MR. PRESIDENT."

Then the capital of the United States was moved to Philadelphia, which was a bigger city than New York. And so the Adams family had to pack up yet again!

Abigail didn't like Philadelphia. Her social duties as wife of the vice president wore on her. The servants were not up to her standards. She fired seven cooks! And John was not happy with his new job . . . there wasn't enough for the vice president to do.

In May 1791 John and Abigail returned to Braintree. Abigail was sick with a fever all summer. It was probably a disease caught from mosquitoes in New York. In October it was back to Philadelphia, but soon Abigail returned to Peacefield, sick again.

In 1792 George Washington won a second term as president. John Adams was vice president again for the next four years. Abigail stayed home in Massachusetts. It was a way to save money.

John Adams no longer needed the big house in Philadelphia, nor did the vice president entertain nearly as much when his wife wasn't there. Every spring John could come home to read and farm until the fall.

Of course, John and Abigail wrote to each other whenever they were apart. Abigail was getting more and more interested in politics. Political parties were beginning to form. John was a Federalist who believed in a strong central government. Thomas Jefferson, on the other hand, belonged to the Democratic-Republican Party. It believed that the people should have the power, and a weak government was best.

In 1796 George Washington decided not to run for a third term as president. The big question now for Abigail and John Adams was whether John should run for president against Thomas Jefferson. It would be a bitter fight. Jefferson and the Adamses were no longer friends, because their political beliefs were so different. Abigail knew that her husband would be attacked by political enemies. The attacks hurt her as much as him. It would also be hard to follow a great man like George Washington. She worried about John's age (sixty-one) and health. Abigail dreaded going back to Philadelphia and having to do all that entertaining. She wondered if she would be able to keep quiet in political arguments. She had strong views, and it would be difficult not to voice them. Martha Washington was a tough act to follow. Abigail thought she had acted perfectly as the wife of the first president.

MARTHA WASHINGTON

John was unsure about running. But in the end, Abigail thought he should . . . and he won, but just barely.

Chapter 8
Mrs. President

Abigail couldn't be in Philadelphia in 1797 when her husband was sworn in as the second president of the United States. She was caring for John's eighty-nine-year-old mother, who would die in her arms.

John begged Abigail to join him. He wrote, "I never wanted your Advice and assistance more in my Life." Abigail had avoided Philadelphia for five years, and she dreaded the exhausting trip on terrible, muddy roads.

But when Abigail arrived she swung into action! She got up at 5:00 a.m. to write letters, plan the day, and organize the servants. Breakfast was at eight. She saw guests from eleven to two and had dinner with the family at three. After that she visited wives of men in the government until sundown. In the evening she held dinners for important people. She also organized giant celebrations for New Year's Day and July Fourth. Despite her full days, she still remained the president's advisor. Her husband said, "I can do nothing without you."

She was so involved, people called her "Mrs. President."

As Abigail feared, the presidency came with many problems. One was the threat of war with France. While trying to reason with the French, John created the Department of the Navy. Abigail thought he should declare war, but John disagreed. Within the United States, John was under constant attack from his political enemies, no matter what he did. Their harsh words were misery for Abigail. She thought criticizing the president was treason, even when she agreed with the criticism!

During the summer of 1798, while at home at Peacefield, Abigail fell so sick she feared she might die. John was home with her and said it was the "most gloomy summer" of his life. Abigail was still not well when John had to go back to Philadelphia without her in the fall. But as soon as she felt better, Abigail was able to supervise the building of a new barn.

When Abigail finally joined John in Philadelphia, she brought their son Thomas, their daughter Nabby, and Nabby's daughter Caroline.

Another election was coming up soon. Abigail feared that her husband wouldn't win a second term as president in 1800. She knew that he would take defeat very personally.

Then in December 1799, George Washington died at age sixty-seven. The whole country went into mourning. He was known as the father of the country. Indeed, people felt that they had suffered a personal loss. Abigail said, "No man ever lived more deservedly beloved and respected."

A new capital city, Washington, was planned in his honor. Washington was much farther south, near Virginia. A new house for the president was being built there. It later became known as the White House.

THE PRESIDENT'S HOUSE

BUILDING OF THE PRESIDENT'S HOUSE BEGAN IN 1792 AND WAS DONE MOSTLY BY SLAVES AND IMMIGRANTS. IT TOOK EIGHT YEARS, AND IT STILL WASN'T FINISHED WHEN THE ADAMSES MOVED IN.

THE ORIGINAL BUILDING WAS SUPPOSED TO BE THREE STORIES HIGH AND MUCH BIGGER, BUT ITS SIZE HAD TO BE CUT BACK BECAUSE OF SHORTAGES OF MATERIALS AND LABOR. THE HOUSE WAS ORIGINALLY CALLED "THE PRESIDENT'S

PALACE" OR "THE PRESIDENT'S HOUSE," BUT IN TIME PEOPLE CALLED IT "THE WHITE HOUSE" BECAUSE OF ITS WHITEWASHED COLOR.

IN 1814, DURING THE WAR OF 1812, THE BRITISH RANSACKED AND BURNED DOWN THE WHITE HOUSE. NOTHING WAS LEFT EXCEPT THE OUTSIDE WALLS, AND THEY HAD TO BE TORN DOWN. IT TOOK ONLY TWO YEARS TO REBUILD. IT WAS FINISHED IN 1817, THOUGH THERE HAVE BEEN MANY ADDITIONS TO IT SINCE THEN.

The Adamses went home for the summer and made more additions to Peacefield. In the fall of 1800 John moved to the new president's house in Washington, and Abigail followed. However, on the way there, Abigail's carriage got lost in the wilderness, and it took an extra day to arrive. When she finally did, she saw that Washington was not much more than a village in a swamp. Abigail was taken aback. "It is the very dirtiest Hole I ever saw . . . a quagmire after every Rain."

The house was unfinished, cold, and damp, even with fires roaring in thirteen fireplaces. Abigail hung clothes to dry in the East Room.

The Adamses didn't know if they would live there for only a few months or four years. The presidential election would be held in December. John was not a popular leader. Some people thought he was vain and wanted to be like a king (which John strongly denied). He was known to be stubborn and too opinionated. It was looking

like the Adamses' stay in Washington might be short.

John Adams did lose the election, just as Abigail feared, to Thomas Jefferson. Both John and Abigail felt humiliated and angry.

On top of the defeat, in 1800 they heard that their son Charles had died. It was a terrible blow. Charles was only thirty years old. Abigail was especially sad, because Charles had been such a charming child. But his life had been destroyed by drinking.

The only good news was that war with France had been avoided. John had worked hard for that. People had thought that war was a sure thing. John was very proud of maintaining peace. It was the greatest achievement of John Adams's presidency.

After only three months in Washington, Abigail happily left for Peacefield. John followed a few weeks later. He had missed too much family life. "I must be a farmer," he said. And that was just what he became.

Abigail and John didn't need to write any more letters to each other ever again.

Chapter 9
Peacefield

Abigail and John were so happy to be home. They took great pleasure in running the farm. They were surrounded by friends and relatives and grandchildren. There were often as many as twenty people living with them! John and Abigail loved the commotion. On Sundays Abigail cooked a big dinner.

For a while all of their grandchildren were living with them except for John Quincy Adams's child. That was because John Quincy was serving as minister to Russia. Abigail didn't like for her son to be so far away, and she was afraid of never seeing him again. It was 1809, and James Madison was president. Abigail wrote to President Madison saying that John Quincy wanted to come home.

President Madison wisely told her that he wouldn't bring John Quincy home unless he heard so from John Quincy himself!

Although practically the entire Adams family was together, the happy times did not last. Abigail's dear sister Mary and her husband died. John Quincy in Russia had a one-year-old daughter who died. Now all of Abigail and John's children had lost children of their own.

Worst of all for Abigail, Nabby developed breast cancer. She had surgery without any anesthesia. The pain must have been almost unbearable. How hard for Abigail to watch her daughter suffer. Nabby spent a year at Peacefield getting better. Then she moved to New York. In time, the breast cancer came back. Terribly weak, Nabby made the trip back to Peacefield and died there. She was forty-eight years old.

Losing her dear daughter and companion was heartbreaking. Nabby's death aged Abigail greatly.

People said she became an old woman. Sometimes it was hard for her to write because the pain in her hands hurt so much.

Abigail complained that her memory was failing, but she stayed very interested in politics. This time, the War of 1812 was on her mind. The United States was at war with England again. The British burned the Capitol building and the president's house in Washington. Although far away, Abigail was outraged. She thought the war against England was right and necessary. When the minister in her church gave a sermon against the war, Abigail stopped going to church!

When the war ended in 1814, John Quincy was sent to London to work on the peace treaty with Great Britain. Abigail and John were very proud of their son. Later, when he became secretary of state, they were even prouder.

Abigail and John celebrated their fiftieth wedding anniversary in 1814 with a big supper.

Abigail said, "I have great cause for thankfulness."

Even so, many of their old friends and relatives had died. Both of Abigail's younger sisters had died. In 1816 John and Abigail were sick all winter. They were both feeling very old. Abigail still managed to have a good attitude about life. "I always thought a laughing philosophy much wiser than a sniveling one," she wrote to her son John Quincy.

In October 1818 Abigail got typhoid fever. It is spread from person to person. It was yet another frightening disease common in Abigail's time. She told John and others by her bedside that she didn't want to live longer if she wasn't useful. She died on October 28 at age seventy-three. John, her "dearest friend," wished he could die with her, but he lived eight more years to age ninety.

A little over six years after Abigail died, her son John Quincy Adams became the sixth president of the United States. John, his father, was joyful, but

THE WAR OF 1812

THE UNITED STATES DECLARED WAR ON GREAT
BRITAIN IN 1812. IT IS SOMETIMES CALLED THE
"SECOND WAR OF INDEPENDENCE." THE BRITISH
WERE TRYING TO KEEP AMERICANS FROM BUYING
OR SELLING GOODS TO FRANCE. THEY ALSO
WANTED TO STOP AMERICA FROM TAKING OVER
INDIAN LANDS AND PARTS OF CANADA. BATTLES
WERE FOUGHT ON LAND, SEA, RIVERS, AND LAKES.
THE UNITED STATES WAS DEFEATED MANY TIMES BY

THE BRITISH AND THEIR INDIAN ALLIES DURING THE WAR. WASHINGTON, DC, WAS BURNED IN AUGUST 1814. ONE BATTLE IN BALTIMORE INSPIRED THE WORDS TO "THE STAR SPANGLED BANNER." A TREATY WAS FINALLY SIGNED IN DECEMBER 1814. NEITHER SIDE GAINED OR LOST TERRITORY IN THE WAR. AND FROM THAT TIME ON, THERE HAS BEEN A LASTING PEACE AND FRIENDSHIP BETWEEN GREAT BRITAIN AND THE UNITED STATES.

said, "How proud she would have been." Abigail was the wife of one US president and the mother of another.

More important, she was always a wonderful wife and mother. She lived in interesting times and influenced American history with her ideas. She believed in the power of education and spoke out for the rights of women and African Americans.

In those times, women didn't leave wills, because their property was their husband's. But Abigail left a will, a most unusual one. She was fair to her sons, but made sure her granddaughters, female cousins, nieces, and female servants got a share as well. Even in death, she tried to right the unfairness that society had placed upon women.

PRESIDENT JOHN QUINCY ADAMS

DURING HIS TERM AS PRESIDENT FROM 1825 TO 1829, JOHN QUINCY ADAMS MANAGED TO MAKE THE AMERICAN ECONOMY STRONGER. HE TRIED TO IMPROVE ROADS, PORTS, AND CANALS TO LINK DIFFERENT PARTS OF THE COUNTRY TOGETHER. LIKE HIS MOTHER, HE PUSHED FOR BETTER EDUCATION. HE WANTED TO SEE A NATIONAL UNIVERSITY. HE WANTED THE GOVERNMENT TO INVEST MORE IN SCIENCE AND ART. UNFORTUNATELY, JOHN QUINCY WAS NOT MUCH OF A POLITICIAN, AND HE COULDN'T GET CONGRESS TO GO ALONG WITH MANY OF HIS IDEAS. NO WONDER ADAMS WAS KNOWN TO DISLIKE BEING PRESIDENT. HE LOST THE ELECTION OF 1828 TO ANDREW JACKSON. JOHN QUINCY STAYED IN POLITICS, AND IN 1831 HE JOINED CONGRESS AS A MEMBER OF THE HOUSE OF REPRESENTATIVES.

TIMELINE OF
ABIGAIL ADAMS'S LIFE

1744	Born on November 11 in Weymouth, Massachusetts
1759	Meets her future husband, John Adams
1764	Marries John Adams on October 25
1765	Nabby (Abigail Amelia) is born
1767	John Quincy is born
1768	Susanna is born
1770	Susanna dies; Charles is born
1772	Thomas is born
1775	Abigail's mother dies
1776	Abigail sends her "Remember the Ladies" letter to John
1777	Elizabeth is stillborn
1783	Abigail's father dies
1784	Travels to Europe with Nabby
1785	Travels to Great Britain with John and Nabby
1786	Nabby marries
1787	Abigail is a grandmother when Nabby's son is born
1788	Travels home with John to Braintree (Quincy), Massachusetts
1789	John is vice president of the US for two terms
1797	John is second president of the US
1798	Abigail seriously ill and nearly dies
1800	Moves into the White House; son Charles dies
1801	Returns to Peacefield in Quincy
1813	Nabby dies
1818	Abigail dies of typhoid fever in Quincy on October 28

TIMELINE OF THE WORLD

George Washington is born	1732
John Adams is born	1735
Thomas Jefferson is born	1743
French and Indian War begins	1754
George III becomes King of England	1760
The Boston Massacre	1770
The Boston Tea Party	1773
First Continental Congress in Philadelphia	1774
The American Revolution begins; Battle of Lexington and Concord; Battle of Bunker Hill; Second Continental Congress	1775
The Declaration of Independence is signed	1776
The British surrender at Yorktown	1781
American Revolution ends with the Treaty of Paris	1783
The US Constitution goes into effect; George Washington is the first American president; John Adams becomes vice president; French Revolution begins	1789
John Adams becomes president	1797
George Washington dies	1799
Thomas Jefferson becomes president	1801
The War of 1812 between the US and Britain	1812
John Quincy Adams becomes sixth president of the US	1825
Thomas Jefferson and John Adams die on July 4	1826
Andrew Jackson becomes president	1829
John Quincy Adams dies	1848
Women in the US gain the right to vote	1920

BIBLIOGRAPHY

BOOKS

* Bober, Natalie S. **Abigail Adams: Witness to a Revolution.** Atheneum Books for Young Readers, New York, 1995.

Holton, Woody. **Abigail Adams.** Free Press, New York, 2009.

Levin, Phyllis Lee. **Abigail Adams: A Biography.** St. Martin's Griffin, New York, 2001.

McCullough, David. **John Adams.** Simon and Schuster, New York, 2001.

* St. George, Judith. **John and Abigail Adams: An American Love Story.** Holiday House, New York, 2001.

* Sawyer, Kem Knapp. **DK Biography: Abigail Adams.** DK Publishing, New York, 2009.

* Wallner, Alexandra (illustrator and author). **Abigail Adams.** Holiday House, New York, 2001.

WEBSITES

whitehouse.gov/about/first-ladies/abigailadams

pbs.org/wgbh/amex/adams

firstladies.org/biographies/firstladies.aspx?biography=2

cr.nps.gov/nr/travel/wash/dc76.htm

nps.gov/history/nr/travel/wash/dc31.htm

To read some of Abigail's letters:
familytales.org/results.php?tla=aba

See also, just for fun:
John Adams (miniseries, starring Laura Linney and Paul Giamatti), HBO, 2008.

* Books for young readers